Sky above,
sand below,
peace within.

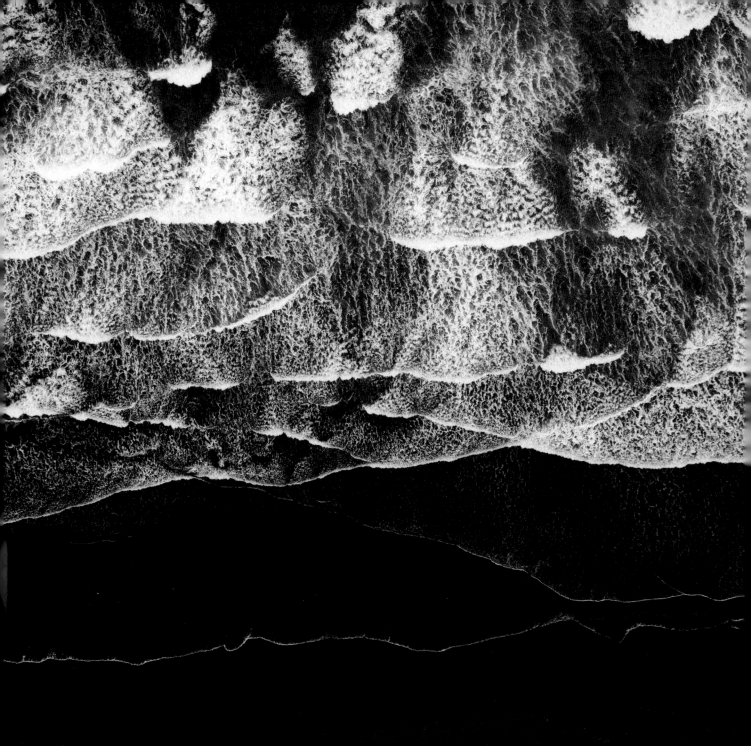

We ourselves feel what we are doing is just a drop in the ocean. But the ocean would be less because of that missing drop.

Mother Teresa

We are like islands in the sea, separate on
the surface but connected on the deep.

William James

The sea does not like to be restrained.
Rick Riordan

At night, time becomes a calm
sea. It goes on for ever.

Francoise Sagan

We dream in colors borrowed from the sea.
Unknown

The waves of the sea help
me get back to me.
Unknown

The heart of man is very much like the sea,
it has its storms, it has its tides and in its
depths it has its pearls too.

Vincent van Gogh

There's nothing more beautiful than the way the ocean refuses to stop kissing the shoreline, no matter how many times it's sent away.

Sarah Kay

To reach a port we must set sail.
Sail, not tie at anchor. Sail, not drift.

Franklin D. Roosevelt

Together we can face challenges as deep
as the ocean and as high as the sky.

Sonia Gandhi

Individually, we are one drop.
Together, we are an ocean.

Ryunosuke Satoro

"Dance with the waves, move with the sea, let
the rhythm of the water set your soul free.

Christy Ann Martine

Life is like the ocean,
it goes up and down.

Vanessa Paradis

The sea, once it casts its spell, holds
one in its net of wonder forever.

Jacques Cousteau

We are tied to the ocean. And when we go back
to the sea, whether it is to sail or to watch – we
are going back from whence we came.

John F. Kennedy

The ocean stirs the heart, inspires the imagination and brings eternal joy to the soul.

Robert Wylan

If the ocean can calm itself, so can you.
We are both salt water mixed with air.

Nayyirah Waheed

The cure for anything is salt water:
sweat, tears or the sea.

Isak Dinesen

There must be something strangely sacred
in salt. It is in our tears and in the sea.

Khalil Gibran

Why do we love the sea? It is because it has some potent power to make us think things we like to think.

Robert Henri

If you want to hear the distant voice of the ocean
put your ear to the distant lips of a seashell.

Curtis Tyrone Jones

you will love the ocean. It makes you feel small, but not in a bad way. Small because you realize you're part of something bigger.

Lauren Myracle

Water always goes where it wants to go, and
nothing, in the end, can stand against it. Water
is patient. Dripping water wears away a stone.
Margaret Atwood

For whatever we lose, it's always
our self we find in the sea.

E.E. Cummings

Let the waves carry you
where the light can not.

Mohit Kaushik

The sea does not like to be restrained.

Rick Riordan

The sea has boundless patience.

Craig Robertson

With every drop of water you drink, every breath you take, you're connected to the sea. No matter where on earth you live.

Sylvie Earle

In one drop of water are found
all the secrets of all the oceans.

Kahlil Gibran

A smooth sea never made a skilled sailor.
Franklin D. Roosevelt

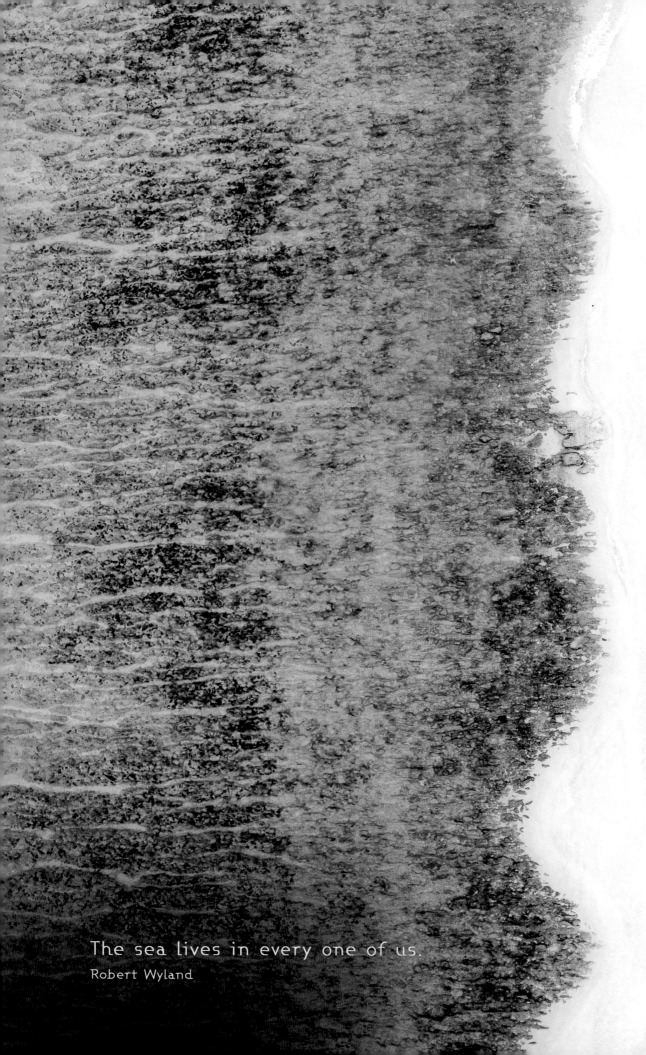

The sea lives in every one of us.
Robert Wyland

I wanted freedom, open air and
adventure. I found it on the sea.
Alain Gerbeault

Smell the sea and feel the sky,
let your soul and spirit fly.

Van Morrison

Live in the sunshine, swim
the sea, drink the wild air.

Ralph Waldo Emerson

I need vitamin sea.

Unknown

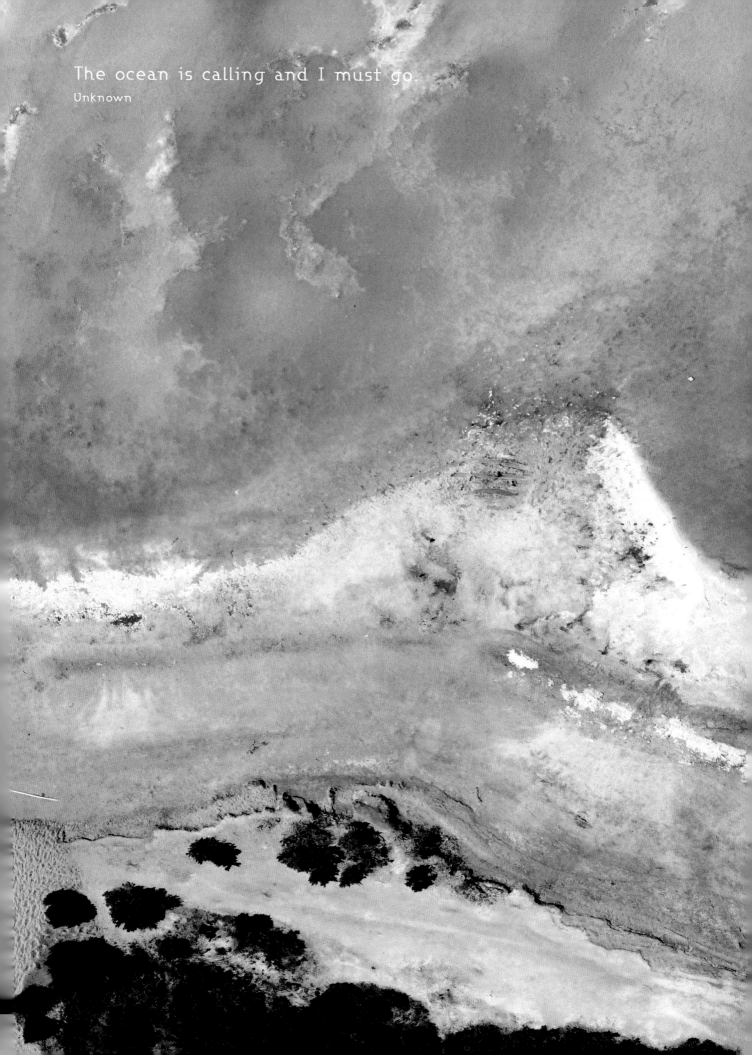

The ocean is calling and I must go.
Unknown

Let the waves carry you
where the light can not.

Mohit Kaushik

Sometimes in the waves of change,
we find our true direction.

Unknown

Let the sea set you free.
Unknown

A rising tide lifts all boats.
Sean Lemass

A lot of people attack the sea, I make love to it.

Jacques Cousteau

How foolish to believe we are more powerful than the sea or the sky.

Ruta Sepetys

A rough day at sea is better
than any day in the office.

Unknown

The sea is a desert of waves,
A wilderness of water.

Langston Hughes

The sea is as near as we come to another world.
Anne Stevenson

The ocean is a mighty harmonist.
William Wordsworth

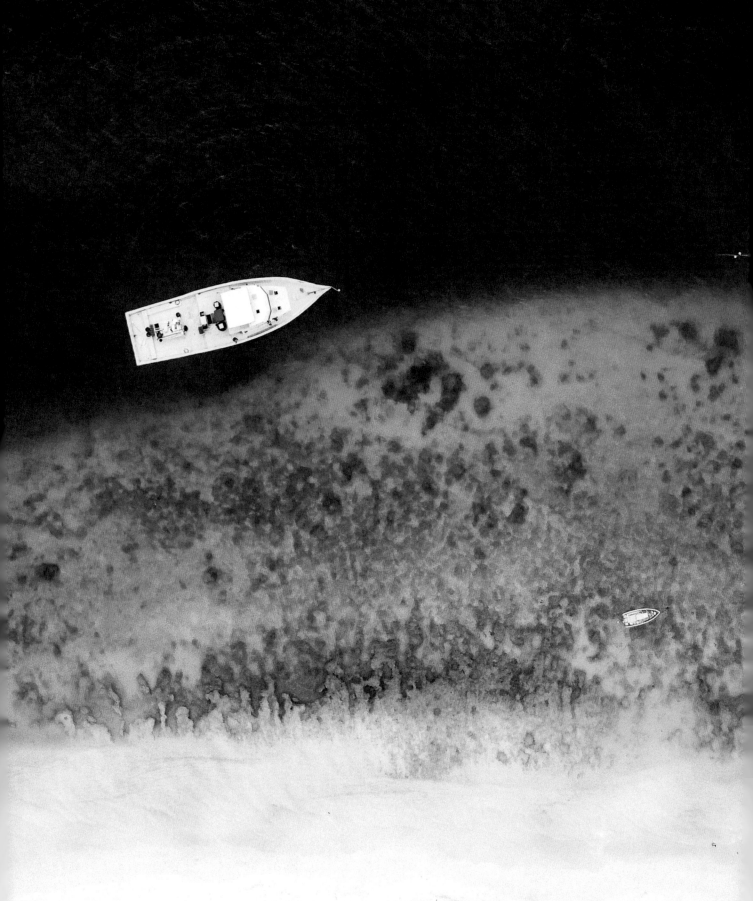

Even the upper end of the
river believes in the ocean.

William Stafford

Eternity begins and ends
with the ocean's tides.

Unknown

A smooth sea never made a skilled sailor.

Franklin D. Roosevelt

We are all in the same boat, in a stormy sea,
and we owe each other a terrible loyalty.

Gilbert K. Chesterton

Rough seas make stronger sailors.
Tough times build greater people.

Robin Sharma

Life is like the ocean. It can be calm or still, and rough or rigid. But in the end, it is always beautiful.

Unknown

Great sea captains are made in rough waters and deep seas.

Kathryn Kuhlman

The human heart is like a ship on a stormy
sea driven about by winds blowing from all
four corners of heaven.

Martin Luther

Family is a life jacket in the stormy sea of life.

J.K. Rowling

What world lies beyond that stormy sea I
do not know, but every ocean has a distant
shore, and I shall reach it.

Cesare Pavese

Life's roughest storms prove
the strength of our anchors.

Unknown

But where, after all, would be the poetry
of the sea were there no wild waves?

Joshua Slocum

The roaring of lions, the howling of wolves, the raging of the stormy sea, and the destructive sword, are portions of eternity, too great for the eye of man.

William Blake

There are some things you learn
best in calm, and some in storm.

Willa Cather

Ships are safe in harbor, but that's not what ships
are for. So set sail on the stormy sea of love.
You're going to get soaked at times, but at least
you'll know you're alive.

Dan Millman

The courage to press on regardless
is the quintessential attribute of
the successful investor.

John C. Bogle

In a calm sea, every man is a pilot.

John Ray

No matter how rough the sea, I refuse to sink.

Unknown

Storms draw something out of us
that calm seas don't.

Bill Hybels

But never have I been a blue calm
sea. I have always been a storm.

Stevie Nicks

Great people are not affected by each puff of
wind that blows ill. Like great ships, they sail
serenely on, in a calm sea or a great tempest.

George Washington

It is extraordinary to see the sea; what a spectacle!
She is so unfettered that one wonders whether it is
possible that she again become calm.

Claude Monet

The man who has experienced
shipwreck shudders even at a
calm sea.

Ovid

Instead of passing on choppy waters to
the next generation, we should endeavour
to leave them a calmer sea.

Najib Razak

You have to think of your career the way you look at the ocean, deciding which wave you're gonna take and which waves you're not gonna take. Some of the waves are going to be big, some are gonna be small, sometimes the sea is going to be calm. Your career is not going to be one steady march upward to glory.

Alan Arkin

To us large creatures, space-time is like the sea seen from an ocean liner, smooth and serene. Up close, though, on tiny scales, it's waves and bubbles. At extremely fine scales, pockets and bubbles of space-time can form at random, sputtering into being, then dissolving.

Gregory Benford

If there is magic on this planet,
it is contained in water.

Loren Eiseley

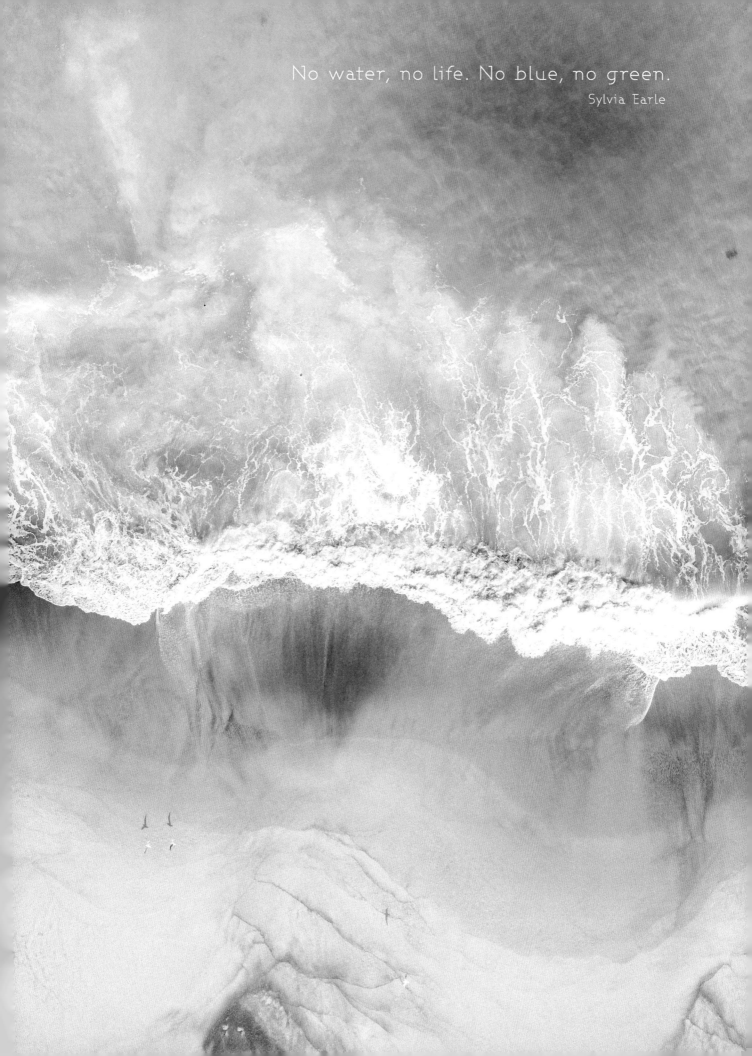

No water, no life. No blue, no green.
Sylvia Earle

Happiness is a day at the beach.
Unknown